Eugene A. Magevney

**The Jesuits as Educators**

Eugene A. Magevney

**The Jesuits as Educators**

ISBN/EAN: 9783744648387

Printed in Europe, USA, Canada, Australia, Japan

Cover: Foto ©Lupo / pixelio.de

More available books at **www.hansebooks.com**

PEDAGOGICAL TRUTH LIBRARY.

❧

# The Jesuits as Educators

❧

..BY THE..

## REV. EUGENE MAGEVNEY, S. J.

### St. Ignatius' College, Chicago, Ill.

❧

NEW YORK:

THE CATHEDRAL LIBRARY ASS'N

123 EAST 50TH STREET

1899

# INTRODUCTION.

———

ENCOURAGED by the cordial reception accorded the initial number of our PEDAGOGICAL TRUTH LIBRARY, "Christian Education in the Dark Ages," we venture to issue its successor from the same polished and eloquent pen. In small compass, without exaggeration, lucidly, forcibly and with erudition, Father Magevney sets forth the history and character of the marvelous system of education embodied in the Jesuit *Ratio Studiorum*. We hope that it will go far to correct erroneous impressions gathered either from the maltreatment or imperfect treatment of the subject in popular pedagogical books. There is so widespread an interest in themes of this sort, and, consequently, so much need of a Catholic presentation of the history of Pedagogy, that the little book will be its own apology. Its graceful style, cultured diction and skilful array of facts will, we are sure, earn for it a warm welcome.

### The Cathedral Library Association

*November 8th, 1899.*

The history of the Society of Jesus has been before the world for centuries, teeming with the eulogy of friends and the aspersion of foes. It is no present purpose of this sketch to take up either strain, but simply to describe in a few brief words some leading features of the teaching .system of the Order. As an educational institution, the Society has occupied a prominent place at all times ; exercised a wide range of influence upon the intellectual destiny of . millions, and contributed in no small degree to the revival and steady advancement of Letters. (Its founder, Inigo de Loyola, was a chivalric Spanish Knight of the sixteenth century, who fell wounded by a cannon ball when fighting for his country in the breach at Pampeluna. The occurrence, apparently so casual, turned the whole tide of his thought and life into other and deeper channels. When recovered from the long confinement, incident upon his mishap, he resolved to figure no more in the ranks of Spain as a champion of her ancient glory. but to devote himself wholly to the enlargement of the realms of Christian civilization. But how was he to affect this? Such was the question which he put to himself, and which he pondered long and diligently before he ventured upon an answer. At last it occurred to him that no means could be more efficacious than the widespread diffusion of knowledge through the instrumentality of education as sound as it was broad. The general condition of the times, if nothing else, would have led him to this conclusion. The Reformation had but lately dawned. Controversy was running riot. The man of mind was the man of the hour, and he felt that if he would prove successful as a defender of the Church and win his way deep into human conviction, mental equipment of a high and varied character was imperatively demanded. He would, therefore, organize a body of men, one of the leading purposes of whose institution would be to train the young. To invest that training with the proper thoroughness he would summon to his aid, as far as possible, none but men of multiplied and distinguished ability. With this end in view he sought the Paris University, the acknowledged literary centre of his day. His sojourn within its walls not only gave him the amplest opportunity of acquiring for himself that large acquaintance with books which he felt to be needful, but also brought him in frequent contact with many of the keenest intellects of the period. From amongst them it was his wish to win sympathizers and recruits in his undertaking. Seven years came and went—years of preparation, years of organization ; and when upon the expiration of that time, we behold him and his first ten companions grouped about the shrine in the crpyt of Montmartre devoting themselves by vow to their cherished work, we are presented with the first chapter in the history of his realized hopes. The Society of Jesus was born, and another, an eventful page was beginning to be written in the annals of modern education.

Scarcely was the infant Society well established when plans were matured bearing upon the main purpose of its institution. The chief object, and one never lost sight of, was to supply the educational necessities of the times, to make up for the deficiencies of older methods and, as far as practicable, leave nothing undone for the construction of a perfect system. As its numbers increased, colleges immediately sprang up in every quarter of Europe. Additions and emendations dictated by experience were made in the original scheme. Thus the process went on maturing, year after year, during the lifetime of the founder and long after he had passed away, until, under the generalship of Aquaviva, in 1581, it was deemed advisable to frame, once for all, a uniform method of teaching to be made binding upon the entire Order. This was done, and during the years that elapsed before the suppression of the Society in 1773, the learned world had abundant opportunity of gauging it and pronouncing upon its availability as a system. Nor do we hesitate to say, satisfied that we are in line with the facts of the case, that the verdict was preëminently in its favor. Protestants vied with Catholics in the praises which they lavished upon it, and in many cases went far beyond them. So much so, that it will always remain an anomaly, if not rather a providential arrangement, in the history of the Society of Jesus, that, when Catholic princes were clamoring for its annihilation, Catherine of Russia,

4

and Frederick of Prussia, for the educational advantages which it afforded the youth of their respective lands, flung around it the shield of their brave and generous protection. The circumstance was an odd one, and gave occasion to D'Alembert for one of his delicate, satiric thrusts. Writing to Frederick II, apropos of his refusal to join in the royal league against the Jesuits, he says: " It will be curious, Sire, if, while their very Christian, very Catholic, very Apostolic and very Faithful Majesties destroy the grenadiers of the Holy See, your very Heretical Majesty should alone maintain them." Nevertheless he did maintain them, and in a subsequent correspondence with the celebrated infidel, assured him that France would in due time reap the fruit of her folly in suppressing the Society, and that in the first years especially the education of youth would be sadly neglected.[2]

---

(1) Clement XIV et les Jésuites, p. 292.

(2) "I see in them (the Jesuits)," wrote Frederick II to D'Alembert, "only men of letters, whom it would be very difficult to replace for the education of youth. It is this important object which makes them necessary for me" Oeuvres Philosophiques de D'Alembert, Vol. XVIII.
"In time you will experience in France the effects of the destruction of this famous Society ; and during the first years especially, the education of youth will suffer." Ibid. Crétineau Joly, Vol. V., p. 369.

Was it so? It would ill befit us to say.[1] But the overwhelming calamity of the French Revolution which, in the very next generation, broke with such incomparable fury over the face of all Europe, seemed to verify but too literally the awful truth of his prophetic utterance. Scarcely were these hated and hounded guardians of youth off the scene when the flood gates were opened, and with what dire consequences to the world no reader of history need be told. The first generation in France educated out of Jesuit schools was infidel and communistic to the core and aimed at the destruction of throne and altar alike. The spirit and policy of which Danton and Marat, Robespierre and Desmoulins were the fiendish impersonations, were the Dead Sea fruitage of all the hopeful promises that had been made by the Revolutionists on condition that the Society of Jesus were suppressed. Civilization was to have advanced with giant strides. Education was

---

(1) The historian, Dallas, a non-Catholic apologist for the Order, has no doubt of it. He sees in the Revolution and its distressful consequences the only result that could have been expected from the worse than pagan education which had been substituted for Jesuit training. cf. *The New Conspiracy against the Jesuits*, cc. III. IV.

to have been improved as never before. The moral atmosphere was to have been cleansed of the infectious taint with which three centuries of Jesuit intrigue and aggression had befouled it. But, instead, we find in the sequel that the expected millennium never dawned. That the attack had really been made not upon Jesuits alone or even primarily, but through them upon all religion and even upon the fundamental principles of natural right and truth. The social and moral fabrics were jarred to their foundations in the prostituted names of liberty and fraternity, and in support of an unhallowed progress which the Jesuits could well afford to be accused of having striven to impede. Chateaubriand, pondering the wreck and ruin visible in the wake of the receding storm, had every reason to bewail the deplorable condition of things around him and exclaim : "Europe has suffered an irreparable loss in the Jesuits. Education has never since held up her head."[1] And when at the beginning of the present century, iniquity had run its course and a rift was made in the dark cloud

---

(1) Génie du Christianisme. Tom. VIII., p. 199.

overhead, it was not surprising that the nations, particularly those in which the attack upon the Order had been most violent and which, as a consequence, had suffered most, called loudly for its speedy resuscitation. Spain, Portugal and France, Naples and Parma were instant in their demands for its revival. No sooner was it risen from the tomb and Jesuits were once more allowed to resume their wonted avocation as teachers, than a pæan of exultation rang out where but yesterday the strains of a requiem had been heard. Was it surprising? Not at all! It was nothing more than the logic of events working itself out to a foregone conclusion.)

As a natural result of its popularity the educational system of the Jesuits, from the very start, met with acceptance far and wide. Already, within the lifetime of its founder, the Order had set up colleges in France, Spain, Italy and Portugal; while its progress through the German States was a veritable triumphant march. In 1551 the members of the Order had scarcely secured a foothold in Germany, and yet in 1556 their colleges were to be met with scattered throughout Swabia, Fran-

8

conia, Austria, the Rhine Provinces, Bavaria and Bohemia. They conquered us, says Ranke, upon our own ground, in our own homes.[1] After the death of Ignatius we find his followers not only over-running Europe, but plying every sea in quest of distant shores upon which to cast the seed of knowledge. In China and Japan, in America, India and Oceanica ; at the very extremities of the habitable globe we meet with them, and in every case they are teachers. Where circumstances were favorable they operated their system in all its detailed fullness by the erection of colleges and universities ; otherwise, as much of it as the situation would allow. But whether called into requisition entirely or in part ; in the intellectual centres of Europe or the tangled wilds of some remote, primeval forest ; whether to unravel the mysteries of science upon the Chairs of renowned universities, or impart the first elements of doctrine to naked savages, it had features distinctly its own and addressed itself to millions of minds. [Lord Macaulay, whose predilection for Jesuits was

---

(1) History of the Papacy, Vol. I. B. V. ₴ 3. Foster's Translation.

certainly not his capital fault, bears a luminous testimony to the truth of this statement in one of his numerous eloquent dashes. "Before the Order had existed a hundred years," he observes, "it had filled the whole world with memorials of great things done and suffered for the faith. * * * * There was no region of the globe, no walk of speculation or of active life, in which the Jesuits were not to be found. They guided the counsels of kings. They deciphered Latin inscriptions. They observed the motions of Jupiter's satellites. They published whole libraries, controversy, casuistry, history, treatises on Optics, Alcaic Odes, editions of the Fathers, madrigals, catechisms and lampoons. The liberal education of youth passed almost entirely into their hands, and was conducted by them with conspicuous ability. They appear to have discovered the exact point to which intellectual culture can be carried without risk of intellectual emancipation. Enmity itself was compelled to own that in the art of managing and framing the tender mind they had no equals."[1] (Sir James Mackintosh, by

(1) History of England. Vol. II. c. 6.

no means partial to Jesuits, delivers himself in a kindred strain. "They (the Jesuits) cultivated polite literature with splendid success ; they were the earliest, and, perhaps, the most extensive reformers of European education, which, in their schools made a larger stride than it has at any succeeding moment. ; and by the just reputation of their learning, as well as by the weapons with which it armed them, they were enabled to carry on a vigorous contest against the most learned impugners of the authority of the Church. * * * The most famous constitutionalists, the most skillful casuists, the ablest schoolmasters, the most celebrated professors, the best teachers of the humblest mechanical arts, the missionaries who could most bravely encounter martyrdom, or who with most patient skill could infuse the rudiments of religion into the minds of ignorant tribes or prejudiced nations, were the growth of their fertile schools."[1] Our own historian, Bancroft, is not less generous in the praise which he bestows upon them as educators. "Their cloisters, he

(1) Historical View of the Reign of James II. c. 8. *in fine.*

writes, became the best schools in the world."[1] A popularity so widespread and to which so many eminent writers, not a few of them otherwise averse to the Society, have borne a willing and noble testimony, could not have been the result of mere chance or caprice. It stands to reason that it must have been founded upon causes inherent in the system itself. Men of the giant calibre of Bacon, Leibnitz and Grotius, not to mention others of equal note, would never have set upon Jesuit educational methods the seal of their profound approbation, had they not discovered in them, from a close scrutiny of their practical as well as theoretical worth, undeniable claims to admiration and praise.[2] What then, it may be asked,

(1) History of the United States, Vol III. c. 20. First Edition. The entire passage, which is a lengthy one, is interesting, but its citation in full would lead us too far afield for the matter in hand.

(2) Bacon's estimate of Jesuit Schools is well known. "As regards teaching," he says, "this is the sum of all direction—take example by the schools of the Jesuits, for better do not exist. When I look at the diligence and activity of the Jesuits, both in imparting knowledge and moulding the heart, I think of the exclamation of Agesilaus concerning Pharnabazus, 'Since thou art so noble I would thou wert on our side.'" De Dign. et Augm. Scient. Lib. I. ad init.

"J'ai toujours pensé," writes Leibnitz, "qu'on reformerait le genre humain, si l'on réformerait l'éducation de la jeunesse. On ne pourra facilement venir à bout de ce dernier point qu'avec le concours de personnes qui, à la bonne volonté et aux connaissances, joignent

were those claims? How far and in what respect, if at all, was the Jesuit system an advance upon all previous methods? By what warrant is the assertion made that they were "the earliest and, perhaps, the most extensive reformers of European education, which, in their schools made a larger stride than it has at any succeeding moment?" What was its permanent contribution to the fund of pedagogical science, then in its infancy, and now in the full blush of its noon-tide development? Had it any new features to impart, or was it merely a rehabilitation of old forms caught up and glorified far beyond their actual deserts? Let us see.)

I. The boast of the nineteenth century is that it has put education within easy reach of the masses by making it *free*. The circumstance has become a theme of reiterated song as well it may, while pedagogues and politicians never tire ring-

---

encore l'autorité. Les Jésuites pouvaient faire de choses étonnantes, surtout quand je considère que l'éducation des jeunes gens fait en partie l'object de leur institut religieux. Mais, à en juger par ce que nous voyons aujourd'hui, le succés n'a pas pleinement répondu à l'attente, et je suis bien éloigné de penser sur ce point comme Bacon, qui lorsq'il s'agit d'une meilleure éducation, se contente de renvoyer aux écoles des Jésuites." Oeuvres de Liebnitz, Tom. 6, p. 65. cf. etiam Grotius, Hist. B. 3. p. 273.

ing the everlasting changes upon it as "the bulwark of American Liberties" and "the palladium of national existence." No blame to them either. Knowledge is power, and to put it within reach of all, the more effectually to enable them to surmount the difficulties of their state and reap some at least of the intelligent benefits of life, is an achievement of which any man or age can well afford to be proud. Mistakes may indeed be made in its application, but the principle itself of free education is sound and unquestionable. Yet glorious as is the idea, far reaching and all embracing as it is bound to be in its ultimate consequences, it is by no means a thing of latter day invention as is too often erroneously supposed. Already in the eighth century and prior to it we find the Councils of the Church enjoining upon bishops and priests the paramount necessity of establishing within the towns and villages under their jurisdiction schools for the *gratuitous* instruction of youth.[1] Who has not heard of the claustral

---

(1) "The first command the bishops had, to establish at their cathedrals public schools, where scholars should be taught gratis, was in the Assembly of Aix-la-Chapelle, in 789. It was renewed by the Third

schools of early medieval times and the cathedral and seminary schools of later date? What reader of history is not as familiar with the names of Fulda, Cluny and Le Bec as with those of Oxford, Cambridge and Harvard in our own day? Of how much disinterested zeal in the cause of learning are we not reminded by the memories which they conjure up? Yet these schools and a host of others of equal grade and celebrity were free. Multitudes flocked to them, and under the supervision of bishop and monk, men of the ripe and royal stamp of Alcuin, Lanfranc and Anselm, knowledge could be had by the young for the mere asking. True, that knowledge may have been, and, in the light of modern discovery, *was* comparatively elementary. It was not systematized and lacked breadth and definiteness. But for all that it was the best the times

---

Council of Lateran in 1179." Vaughn's Life of Aquinas, p. 77. *Note.*
"Schools for the gratuitous instruction of poor children can be traced back," says Barnard, "to the early days of the Christian Church. Wherever a missionary station was set up, or a bishop's residence or seat was fixed, there gradually grew up a large ecclesiastical establishment, in which were concentrated the means of hospitality for all the clergy, and all the humanizing influences of learning and religion for the diocese or district." Encyclopedia of Education. Kiddle. Article: Public Schools.

afforded and enjoyed the rare privilege of being within everybody's reach. Venerable Bede himself assures us that in some quarters so great was the zeal for the diffusion of learning that the students were not only provided with instruction without charge, but were even supplied, during their stay in the monasteries, with food and books *gratis*. Had this liberal spirit survived the vicissitudes of subsequent years, had the practice of free education, begun so early and pursued with such notable success for so many generations, remained in vogue, there would, in all probability, have been no call for the introduction of the Jesuit system into the world. But such was not the case. With the rise and rapid multiplication of the universities minor educational institutions, claustral, cathedral or otherwise, were gradually overshadowed and disappeared, absorbed into a broader and more pregnant condition of affairs. Learned centres like Paris, Bologna, Salamanca and Padua, henceforth became the intellectual magnets toward which young and old, in quest of knowledge, naturally and necessarily gravitated. Even the monks themselves, wrought upon by the spirit of the hour, left their cloisters for a spell and trooped after their disciples to seek in the shadow of the new institutions that broader and broadening culture which was nowhere else to be acquired, and in which they recognized the harbinger of a coming dawn. From the twelfth to the sixteenth century was emphatically a transitional period, characterized as a consequence by the peculiarities ever incident upon change and revolution. It had its commendable features, of course, and its bad qualities ; its advantages and its disadvantages. Intellectual facilities were vastly improved, but at the same time education ceased to be free as it had been in the claustral and cathedral schools where no teachers had to be paid, nor expensive manuscripts to be purchased. The moral atmosphere, moreover, lost much and eventually all of that healthful purity which had distinguished it in the less pretentious educational institutions of generations previous. When Ignatius came upon the scene in the sixteenth century and found himself mingled with the turbulent and eager throng of thousands surging in and out of the halls of the Paris University, such was the situation by which he was confronted. A close student of the philosophy of life, as written between the lines of human circumstance, he was not slow in detecting the essential flaws in the educational system as he saw it in active operation before him. It suggested a problem which he felt called upon to solve—a condition of things which he would strive to remedy at any and every cost. After long deliberation, his plan of reform resolved itself into an educational scheme which, while competent to supply the intellectual outfit of a university curriculum, would not fail to supplement it by what he deemed to be two all-important requisities. These were, first : to render education free, and next, to safeguard it from the moral contamination to which medieval university life was so wantonly exposed. For the purpose of accomplishing the former of these two designs he assembled around him a body of co-laborers. A society of educators was organized. They pledged themselves to give education *gratis*. Once sufficient foundations, made by an original grant

18

from municipality or wealthy person-
age, had been provided for the mainte-
nance of their colleges and their own
individual support, nothing was
asked or accepted from the students
by way of tuition. " No obligations
or conditions," wrote Ignatius in his
Constitutions, "are to be admitted
that would impair the integrity of
our principle, which is : To give
gratuitously what we have received
*gratis.*"[1] This object was all the
more readily attainable as they were
vowed to poverty which reduced
their personal necessities to a minimum and enabled them to operate
their institutions upon a comparatively economic basis. How econom-
ically, is evinced by more than one
well authenticated fact in their history. As might have been expected
this revival of free education was
welcomed in some quarters, and vio-
lently assailed in others. The people
at large hailed it as a forward movement and a relief. Hitherto de-
barred, for want of means, from all
participation in the advantages of a
university course, the humblest now
saw a way opened to them in another
direction leading up to the same if

(1) Constit. Soc. Jesu, pars IV. c. VII. No. 3.

not greater results, and all for less than the price of a song. As a consequence, we find them crowding the schools of the Jesuits wherever and whenever opened. In such numbers in fact did they come that we can but marvel, as every historian has marvelled, at the phenomenal rapidity with which the schools of the Order multiplied. On the other hand wealthy patrons, recognizing the disinterestedness with which the new teachers gave themselves to their chosen work, and the comprehensive and beneficial nature of the work itself, were not slow in coming forward with numerous and munificent endowments. So much so, that in 1750, somewhat over two centuries from its foundation, the Order possessed 769 educational institutions, of which 157 were Normal Schools for the education and training of future professors, and the rest Colleges and Universities.[1] The number of students attendant upon Jesuit instruction varied, of course, with the cir-

---

(1) "In 1550 the first Jesuit school was opened in Germany. In 1700 the Order possessed 612 Colleges, 157 Normal Schools, 59 Novitiates, 340 residences, 200 missions, 29 professed homes, and 24 universities. The College of Clermont had 3000 students in 1695." Encycl. Brittan. (new) p. 589. Art. Education. Vol. VII.

cumstances of time and place. Allowing, however, for an average attendance of 300 in each college, which is putting it exceedingly low in the majority of cases and exaggerating it in none, we have in 1710, for instance, "a sum total of more than 200,000 students in the collegiate and university grades, all being formed, at a given date, under one system of studies and government, intellectual and moral."[1] Quite a creditable showing, truly, when we bear in mind the age of the Society and the tremendous antagonism developed in certain quarters against it, which vainly sought to defeat its purpose and cripple its progress at every turn. The people rejoiced. Not so the universities. They looked askance upon the new departure and were sorely grieved at the increasing popularity and prosperity of the obnoxious new-comers.[2] Their intru-

(1) Loyola and the Educational System of the Jesuits. By Rev. Thomas Hughes, S.J. Scribner's, 1892, p. 74.

cf. etiam Ratio Studiorum et Institutiones Scholasticæ Societatis Jesu. By G. M. Pachtler, S.J. 3 vols. Berlin. A. Hoffman & Co. *passim*,

(2) "À peine la Compagnie de Jésus," says d'Alembert, "commençait-elle à se montrer en France, qu'elle essaya des difficultés sans nombre pour s'y établir. Les Universités surtout firent les plus grands efforts pour écarter ces nouveaux venus. Les Jésuites s'annonçaient pour enseigner gratuite

sion meant, so it was apprehended, for many a professor in said institutions fewer pupils and smaller perquisites in future. They felt that they now had rivals in the field with whom they would have to shiver many a lance in the lists if they would not be outstripped in general esteem and possibly be deprived of the Chairs they occupied. This spirit of estrangement, which so soon degenerated into open hostility on the part of the universities, met the Society at its very inception and dogged it bitterly throughout its checquered and memorable career ; until, at last, it was afforded the grim satisfaction of mingling its *crucifige* in dismal concert with those of the Jansenists and infidels of the eighteenth century, when they demanded so vociferously, and obtained the temporary overthrow of the Order. The Jesuits gave education, higher and secondary, to all *free ;* and this, we take it,

---

ment; ils comptaient déjà parmi eux des hommes savants et célèbres, supérieurs peut-être à ceux dont les universités pouvaient se glorifier; l'intérêt et la vanité pouvaient donc suffire à leurs adversaires pour chercher de les exclure. On se rappelle les contradictions semblables que les ordres mendiants essuyèrent de ces mêmes universités quand ils voulurent s'y introduire; contradictions fondées à peu près sur les mêmes motifs." Destruction des Jésuites en France, p. 19.

was the first provision in the new system which made it popular. In this assertion we are supported by various authorities of note, Catholic and non-Catholic. To cite two of the latter. Apropos of the point, Leopold Ranke writes : " Whenever a prince or a city had founded one of their colleges, no person needed further to incur expense for the education of his children. They were expressly forbidden to ask or accept remuneration or reward. As were their sermons and Masses, so were their instructions altogether gratuitous. * * * * As men are constituted, this of itself must have aided to make the Jesuits popular, the more so as they taught with great ability and equal zeal."[1] An opinion with which Hallam is perfectly in accord. He says : " They taught gratuitously, which threw, however unreasonably, a sort of discredit upon salaried professors ; it was found that boys learned more from them in six months than in two years under other masters ; and probably for both these reasons, even Protestants sometimes withdrew their children from the or-

---

(1) **History of the Papacy.** Vol. I. B. V. § 3.

dinary gymnasia and placed them in Jesuit Colleges."[1]

II. We have mentioned *Normal Schools*. In the facilities which they afforded and the recuperative strength which they implied, we recognize another cause for the popularity of the Jesuit Schools as also a partial explanation of the "great ability" with which as Ranke affirms they were conducted. As every reader of Jesuit history knows, one of the first provisions made by Ignatius—a provision that was enlarged upon and perfected in later years–was for the thorough education of the members of his Order with a view to the lecture hall or class-room. It was a principal object of solicitude with him at all times. They were to be educators. Such was their profession. They should therefore be abundantly fitted out by varied intellectual equipment for the discharge of academic duties in any and every field of pedagogical exercise to which they might afterwards be assigned. He well knew that the development of youthful character, the reputation of his institutions, and their success

(1) Introduction to the Literature of Europe. Vol. I, p. 256.

or failure at the last depended in the main, if not wholly, upon the antecedent qualifications of the masters in charge. In harmony with this idea the second General Assembly, held nine years after his death, laid it down as an all-important requirement that in every Province of the Order, where feasible, schools for the exclusive education of the younger members of the Society should be erected. In them, as far as means and other circumstances would allow, every accommodation was to be afforded for complete literary and scientific development; and only when that development had been attained and proven by a series of searching examinations was the Jesuit aspirant to attempt to introduce others to the charms of literature or lead them through the intricacies of abstruse speculations. The provisions were still ampler. There were embodied in the Constitution as part of its elaborate framework, detailed regulations both as regards the education of the members themselves, and also the manner in which they were to impart their knowledge to others. In the educational *scheme* of the Order, or *Ratio Studiorum*, as it is usually called, the entire training process is fully and distinctly mapped out. It may not prove uninteresting as it certainly will not be irrelevant, to enumerate a few of its salient features. Limiting our inquiry at present to intellectual cultivation, it is needless to say that preparation for the class-room involves two things—a thorough knowledge of the matter to be communicated, with ease and dexterity in the art of its presentation. Accordingly, we find in the system every provision made for the attainment of these two objects.

As regards the studies to be undertaken by the future professor, we may consider them divided into what, for convenience sake, we may designate as lower and higher, *inferiora et superiora*. A. The *former* embrace a thorough study of Grammar, Humanities and Rhetoric covering a period of two and, if need be, three years. The languages cultivated are the Latin, Greek and vernacular, and they are to be pursued not cursorily, not narrowly, but with all the zest and breadth expected of men destined to become professional adepts. There were a number of reasons for the paramount value which Ignatius and his early associates set upon classical learning, and the zeal with which they desired it to be cultivated by all their followers. They lived in a classical age. Latin was the vehicle of scientific thought the world over. Success, therefore, in any department or direction presupposed acquaintance with it. Besides, it was the language of the Church. Her ritual and theology, the decrees of her Councils, her every official utterance, the incomparable writings of so many of her Doctors and Fathers were couched in it, and must forever remain buried treasures to any one unfamiliar with its secrets. Both it and the Greek had been developed for centuries far beyond any other, and were, by consequence, distinguished by a philological exactness and flexibility of structure to which no other language could lay equal claim. Add to all this the permanent advantages to be derived from the diligent conning of works, Latin or Greek, which represent the bloom and blossom of literary excellence, and hold in rich deposit, unto all times, whatever is loftiest and most desirable in human thought. Proficiency in the vernacular was in like manner to be sought after. They believed that apples of gold should be served upon plates of silver, and that it defeats, partially, if not altogether, the efficacy of ideas to trick them out in the homespun toggery of every-day parlance. Perhaps it was a failing of their time, as it is of ours, with some, to amass knowledge the while they neglect the all-important medium of its communication. The results are disastrous. Thoughts otherwise prolific and operative are thus hampered by the language in which they are clad—language far more suggestive of "English as She is spoke" than of the Addisonian purity of the Elizabethan age. B. The *latter*, or *superiora*, embrace a full course of Philosophy, Theology, Physical Science, and Mathematics. Whatever cognate studies are found available for the complete elucidation of the main branches are likewise put under contribution. Scripture, Canon Law, Hebrew, Oriental Languages, and Ecclesiastical History enter as integral parts into the theological curriculum, as Geology, Astronomy, Chemistry and Mechanics do into the philosophical. Seven years, with four hours of lecture a day, are allowed for this course which may be and is, at times, extended to nine or ten in behalf of those whose intellectual qualifications would seem to warrant their being given advanced facilities for improvement. Each year closes with an examination upon the matter traversed, its length and stringency increasing as the student advances. By way of finish to the entire proceeding a thorough examination covering the field of seven years is required. The candidate's future grade in the Order as well as his general availability for the pedagogical work of the Society are to be determined by the greater or less success with which he runs this gauntlet through seven years of stress and difficulty. The preparatory life of the young Jesuit is therefore briefly told. From the moment of his entrance the current of his thoughts and energies and aspirations is made to set in the direction of the class-room where he is one day to dispense the fruits of his present garnering. He is required before admission to have finished at least his *Rhetoric* or what is known as

29

*Junior Class* in our modern under-graduate courses. His literary studies in the Order are consequently something of a repetition, but not altogether so. He now attacks his classics like a man, with a definite aim in life, and with capacities sufficiently enlarged to enable him to compass the depth and breadth of subjects with a penetration and fullness of which he was incapable as a mere youth. The cultivation of style in the three languages; the gauging of authors to be read, memorized and estimated; the manner of analysing and imitating them skillfully—these are the constant objects of his striving during this period of literary formation. Aided by maturing years and the hourly supervision and direction of experienced Masters in literature, and building up upon a closely knit system, his literary instincts and appreciations are elevated and widened, his tastes multiplied, his judgments strengthened, the channel of his thoughts deepened, and it only remains to systematize his ideas by giving them a scientific trend and basis. For this purpose, after graduation in *Letters* and before he enters upon his *Re-*

*gency* or Professorship, he is put to his philosophy. During the three years devoted to it, he covers the entire field of mental and moral Philosophy. Physics, Chemistry and Mathematics, with Astronomy and Geology enter as intercalar branches. Except in the case of Natural Sciences, the lectures, repetitions and text-books are all in the Latin language. The peculiar genius of the Latin, coupled with its uncommon fertility and pliability, renders it a most effective instrument with which to bandy metaphysical niceties. The System of philosophy adhered to, though all are closely scrutinized, is the *Scholastic System;* which means, of course, Aristotle as a basis, purged of his pagan dross in the alembic of Christian interpretation. Collateral branches are not treated as isolated studies. All knowledge is kin, and it is deemed of vital importance never to overlook the fact. Hence the ramifications and interlacings of thought, be they ever so countless and delicate, are assiduously traced and pointed out. Where Metaphysics trench upon Natural Science, or vice versa, due regard is paid to the claims of each, and the law of subor-

31

dination is promptly asserted and vindicated. Naturally enough ; for how diverse soever its manifestations, truth, in its last analysis, is essentially one and self-consistent, and the concrete fact, rightly interpreted, can never be found at variance with the abstract principle. This is a cardinal tenet of the method —a method all the more valuable in an age which tabooes the philosophy of the Schoolmen as a tangled web of medieval extravagances long since swept away by the irresistible force of inductive processes of which it is really the substructure and prop. During these years consecrated to science, literary pursuits are interrupted but not wholly neglected. Latin and the vernacular, of course, come in for a large share of daily attention, while an occasional dip of at least one hour every week into Hesiod or Homer, the translation of an ode of Anacreon or a chorus from Euripides amply suffices to keep the student's appetite for Greek amenities always keenly whetted.

Philosophy ended, his term of *Regency* in one of the numerous Colleges of the Order begins. It lasts for five years. Not having completed his *Studia Superiora*, his teaching during this time is confined to the lower forms. Theory is now reduced to practice. Our quondam pupil becomes a Master. Beginning at the lowest rung of the ladder, he ascends with his scholars from class to class; and, as he does so, grounds himself still further in his art by constant application to the matter in hand — supplementing the strictly pedagogical portion of his work, as he is required to do, by a liberal course of private reading suitable to his avocation and upon the lines of previous study. *Discimus docendo.* At the age of twenty-nine or thirty we meet him again, resuming his higher studies, no longer with a view of teaching merely grammar and belles-lettres, but in order to qualify himself to fill with eminence a chair of Scripture, Theology or other science in a university curriculum. Four and perhaps six years are expended upon this portion of his task. As in philosophy, so now upon a higher plane and in another atmosphere the problems of life are to be sifted; the numberless controversies that strew the pages of dogmatic and Patristic theology are to be faced, and, without a doubt, the vexed questions with which his exegetical studies in particular are rife make constant and heavy demands upon his time and talent. That time and talent, however, are willingly devoted. When his Course is at last finished, he enters for a searching examination in what may be called the work of a lifetime. Success entitles him to the Doctorate, though no degrees are worn by members of the Society. He returns to the Colleges and for the rest of his days holds himself in readiness for the discharge of any pedagogical work, high or low, which may chance to be imposed upon him. Throughout there is nothing eclectic. All is of the strictest obligation, and, saving unavoidable exceptions, every member is put through the same mill.

(To heap up knowledge is one thing; to understand how to communicate it to others in a school-room is a widely different affair, though equally to be cared for in any Normal System worthy of the name. It has not been forgotten in the Jesuit method. On the contrary, it has been provided for variously. In one sense it may be said that a young

Jesuit's entire course of studies is an uninterrupted lesson in the art of teaching. The branches which he studies are the same he will have to expound to the world. He sees in every day's lecture how the subject is to be handled. Its treatment by his professor is full of suggestiveness to him of the manner in which he himself will be expected to deal with it later on.) Let us illustrate this by an example from the department of literature. An oration of Cicero, we may suppose, or an extract from Herodotus is up for consideration. Conformably with the requirements of the *Ratio*, the professor must not quit the subject until he has analyzed it thoroughly and satisfied himself that his pupils have grasped his analysis in all its length and breadth. To insure this result the more effectually, they are required to jot down for future reference whatever is of special value or most apt to slip their memories. Every *word* of importance is examined separately. Its derivation, composition, shade of meaning in different connections, present grammatical bearings and whole influence upon the sentence, perhaps upon the entire speech or chapter, are diligently canvassed and explained. Each *sentence* is closely scrutinized. Its classification, parts, syntactical structure, regular and irregular features, its strength or weakness, cohesiveness or looseness in the context, with a running commentary upon its value as a bit of style are all given, to be afterwards studied, repeated, and committed to writing if need be. The *rhetorical character* of the subject is then passed in review. Its excellences and defects are shown. In what it is deserving of imitation and how one is to proceed in an attempt to imitate it are minutely detailed. Finally, whatever pertains to *erudition* is discussed at length. Mythological, biographical, historical and geographical references are noted and explained. A sketch of the life and character of the author with an account of the part played by the work itself in the march of literary development are furnished. Its worth as compared or contrasted with other productions of the same author or with the works of other writers in the same field is dwelt upon. This analytical study of the subject made by the professor in the presence of his pupils and carefully observed by them, marks distinctly the lines upon which they are, later on, to develop subjects for themselves, as well as the manner in which they are to present them to their own scholars. Besides, there is nothing disorderly or changeful in the analysis itself. The method is one and the work of each succeeding day is uniform with that of the preceding, so that the pupil *nolens volens* is bound, by dint of sheer repetition if not otherwise, eventually to apprehend the process and make it his own in practice. With such a plan as this pursued in the study of Latin, Greek and the vernacular, and that every day and all day, the young Jesuit is forced into an atmosphere of pedagogical experience, and develops into a pedagogue almost without knowing it—so practical, so systematic, so continuous, so well constructed with reference to the end at which it aims is the educational system upon which he is brought up.

(Nor is this all. Entrusted to the guidance of professional teachers and studying to become a teacher himself, his preceptors were recreant to their duty, did they not avail themselves of every opportunity to give his studies their intended bearing, and to imbue him with all the principles needful for self-guidance in after years. Accordingly, no occasion is lost of pointing out to him, now at length, again incidentally, how he is to open up a subject ; how he is to impart an idea ; what process must be followed in its evolution to make it the more seizable by others ; what illustrations may be adduced to throw light into its dark corners ; how serviceable it may become as an element in the formation of mind and heart and character when properly understood ; what are its resources, theoretical or practical, when probed to its bottom ; what books it would be well to suggest to students afterwards with a view to its complete development and the acquisition of that erudition upon the subject necessary for intellectual prominence. Every occasion is utilized to remind him not only of the importance but also of the sacredness and eternal responsibility of his vocation as a teacher, of the manner in which he should comport himself, and of the zeal and skill he is to exercise in manipulating the delicate susceptibilities of youth in order to the formation of perfect manhood. To insure results yet more and give unmistakable evidence of the same, it has been ordained that those about to begin their *Regency* should, for three or four months before they enter the class-room, be taken in charge privately by some experienced master and thoroughly drilled. Assuming the role of teacher by anticipation, they are to interrogate, explain, correct and dictate, while their critical elders ply them with questions and difficulties and resort to countless means of testing their pedagogical metal. The exercise is to be a daily one and continued for not less than an hour. As is evident, its object is to bring to light in due season not only the student's good qualities as a teacher, but likewise his defects so that they may be eliminated in time and not be intruded upon the school-room to the detriment of scholars and professors alike. Further measures of security are shown in the rules laid down for the General Supervisor of studies or Head Master in each college. Possessed of a wider range or acquaintance with matters collegiate, he is instructed to bring his knowledge and experience to bear upon the formation and proper direction of every member of his Faculty. Allowing for originality and individual traits, which he is always to do, he is, nevertheless, to see that the prescriptions of the *Ratio* are strictly carried out ; that uniformity of method be observed ; that nothing foreign be admitted that could disintegrate the System or render it in the least abortive ; that every teacher is at his post and does his duty, not as an independent unit but as part of a concordant whole. To be certain that the Masters have understood and are observing the rules laid down for them, he is to visit their class-rooms frequently, hear them teach, question the pupils in person, note their progress, and afterwards furnish such help and give such advice to the teacher as he may deem called for by the exigencies of the case. His counsel is to be heeded by the young professor. So important, in fact, is tractability considered in the matter, that persistent unwillingness to obey and be guided would expose the offender to permanent forfeiture of position. In a Normal System so elaborate in point of fact, but whose dimmest outlines only we have been able to trace, we recognize the source of two great advantages accruing to the Jesuit method. First of all, it awakened public confidence. Parents were satisfied that their children were not being practiced upon by incompetent tyros, but were being brought up at the hands of trained adepts. Besides, it was an invaluable element of strength resident in the Society itself, and bespoke a recuperative and recruiting power which could not but insure a healthful and permanent educational growth. It was the mainspring of vitality within and the most certain guarantee of efficiency without. "As all the members were thus trained as practical teachers, the Order was, soon after its foundation, enabled, wherever a favorable opportunity offered, to call into existence an astonishing number of literary institutions."[1]

III. A consideration of the Normal Schools in vogue in the Society naturally introduces us to an examination of the *System* itself upon which the colleges were operated. To it, in the third place, we believe much of the Order's prosperity was

<hr/>

(1) Encyclopedia of Education. Kiddle. P. 492.

due, as it was an evident improvement upon anything that had previously existed. Until the appearance of the *Ratio* the essential fault in education had been that it lacked *organization*. Between elements and the higher branches there was a gap, not to mention the deficiencies in elements themselves. No complete, systematic provision had been made for literature, and whatever was accomplished in that line had to be largely a matter of private industry on the part of the student. A pupil's sole ambition, in consequence, was to hurry through grammar and, having acquired a working facility in the use of the Latin language, to plunge into logic and devote the rest of his time to the cultivation of metaphysical abstractions. Ignatius recognized the weakness and danger of such a procedure and sought to remedy it by organizing studies in his colleges upon a more connected and rational basis. So important, in fact, did he rate thoroughness in literature that he expressly insisted that none be allowed to pass to their higher studies' until they had first proved that they had attained the requisite competency. His ideas upon the subject were reinforced by others after him until, finally, they assumed definite and expanded shape in the *Ratio* which may be called the first organized Christian system of studies on record.[1] Before the time of Comenius (1592) "the Jesuits alone," says Quick, "had had a complete educational course planned out, and had pursued a uniform method in carrying this plan through."[2] This organ-

(1) "Ce p·ogramme d'Études (*Ratio*) fut imprimé plus d'un siècle avant la *méthode* de Thomassin (1672) pour l·s Collèges des Oratoriens, un siècle et demi avant le *Traité des Études Monastiques* de Mabillon (1691) à l'usage des Bénédictins, et près de deux siècles avant le *Traité des Études* de Rollin (1740) pour l'Université." Rochemonteix. ; Le Collège Henri IV. Vol. 2, p. 2.

(2) *Educational Reformers.* By R. H. Quick, M A., Trinity College, Cambridge. P. 62. *First Edition.* "The most valuable history of education in our mother tongue."—Educational Review, Vol. I, p. 69. Again he observes, "In this particular (that, namely, of organized studies) the Jesuit schools contrasted strongly with their rivals of old, as indeed with the ordinary schools of the present day. The Head Master, who is to the modern English school what the General, Provincial, Rector, Prefect of Studies and *Ratio Studiorum* combined were to a school of the Jesuits, has perhaps no standard in view up to which the boy should have been brought when his school course is complete[1]. The Masters of form teach just those portions of their subject in which they themselves are interested, in any way that occurs to them, with by no means uniform success; so that when two forms are examined with the same examination papers, it is no very uncommon occurrence for the lower to be found superior to the higher. It is, perhaps, to be expected that a course in which uniform method tends to a definite goal would, on the whole, be more successful than one in which a boy has to accustom him·elf by turns to half a dozen different methods, invented at haphazard by individual Masters with different aims in view, if indeed they have any aims at all." Ibid. p. 15.

ization of studies necessitated a supplementary measure of no less importance which calls for at least a passing notice. To operate their system with anything like effect, they needed a full course of graded text-books, and these accordingly they set to writing and editing, as soon as possible, for their own convenience as a very desirable substitute for what Hallam is pleased to stigmatize, when speaking upon the subject, " as the barbarous school books then in use."[1] The Jesuit school system is simple enough. Presupposing elements, the entire curriculum of lower studies is divided into the Course of Grammar consisting of three or four years, and that of literature made up of two. Students are first to be drilled thoroughly in the sense and practice of grammar until sufficient familiarity with Authors has been acquired to enable them to speak and write correctly. The Course of literature then follows. Though generally finished in two years, strictly speaking it is to have no defined limits of duration, but is to be prolonged until the pupils have compassed the end aimed

---

(1) *loc. cit.*

44

at, which is ease and elegance in composition with a general survey of the whole field of Polite Letters. The means adopted by the *Ratio* to render the teaching in the various classes practically as well as theoretically beneficial are numerous and original. Foremost amongst them are what are technically known as the *prælectio, repetitio, exercitatio, concertatio* and the *argumentum scribendi.* A word upon each. The *prælectio* is a preliminary explanation of the precepts in grammar and the extract in the author assigned for the next day's lesson. In it the significance and force and present application of rules are to be hinted at; and, if it be a question of rhetoric instead of grammar, the student should have pointed out to him, in a general way, the direction his analysis should take if it would open up the passage in all its latent wealth of thought and expression. Such an exercise prepares the way for the more intelligent grasp of the lesson by clearing up doubts and difficulties, to the student, perhaps, altogether insurmountable if left to his own unaided resources. Thus toil and oil are both saved. *Repetitio*, as the word indicates, consists in reviewing the matter seen in order to impress it still more indelibly upon the youthful mind. It proceeds upon the supposition that it is better to see little and see it well than to cover a great deal and do it skimpingly. With language, as with all else, where the foundation laid is deep and firm, there is nothing to be feared for the superstructure to be erected. This repetition is threefold. Each day the explanation of the lessons given the preceding day is to be repeated. On Saturdays, the work of the entire week, in all the branches, is rehearsed synoptically. Upon the opening of each year the matter seen the preceding year is briefly reviewed in order to refresh the memories of the students upon subjects all important in the Course, and which presumably are beginning to grow dim if they have not been already obliterated from the mind. Such continual repetitions besides insuring the knowledge acquired, keep the teacher always in touch with the actual condition of each pupil, enabling him to detect at every stage of the proceedings what the weakness and drawbacks are in each individual case ; to what quarter a stimulus is to be applied; and what should be its nature and extent. The *Exercitatio* is a written exercise done in the school-room by each pupil and under the immediate supervision of the Master. Besides serving as a relief from the tedium of ordinary routine, it awakens interest by reason of the greater mental concentration to which it gives rise, and habituates a youth to the necessary practice of marshalling and managing his own ideas. The *Concertatio* differs from it in being oral and performed either in the class-room or upon a stage publicly. Both are in a measure forms of *repetitio*, but are possessed of features which call for a still larger display of originality, precision and finish. These class tournaments, or *concertationes*, occur between boys of different classes, or those of the same class drawn up in imaginary battle array, in opposing "camps," and seeking to rout one another in recitations and bear off the honors at stake for their "side." As a play upon the ambition of youth, few practices have been found more useful.[1] The *Argumentum*

(1) Educational Reformers. *ut supra.* Appendix. 1. *Class Matches.*

*scribendi* is the outline of a theme or composition dictated to the scholars and upon which their development and elucidation of the matter are to be built. As its purpose would indicate, it is to be diligently prepared by the teacher and in every way suited to the grade of the class and the capacity of the students. Let him even aim at elegance, says the *Ratio*, in its construction, making it a lively and suggestive reproduction of the graceful features of the Authors being read in class. Composition is held in such high esteem by the *Ratio* that proficiency in it, whatever be the language or class, is made the touchstone of success and promotion. How advantageous this practice is as a help thereunto is obvious, since it familiarizes the pupil with the double use of the analytic and synthetic methods of study, and accustoms him, even imperceptibly, to habits of exact thought, so indispensably needful for the simplification and co-ordination of topics. Later he will do the work for himself. At present he requires help. Passing from the lower to the upper or higher studies, those, namely, proper to a university curriculum and to which the Society is to apply itself more especially, there is an easing off, as might well be expected, in the methods of procedure, if not in the work itself. Lecturing is substituted for the explanations customary in the lower forms. Repetitions, though retained, are adapted to the more advanced capacities of the students and the higher character of the studies. Philosophical, theological and other scientific disputations take the place of the *exercitatio* and *concertatio*, while written dissertations upon the matter treated are substituted for the composition work of earlier years. No incitement to study other than zeal for self-improvement and the iron-clad qualifications requisite for graduation are now deemed necessary. Numerous and severe tests are made before degrees in any faculty are granted, and each student must stand or fall by the greater or less diligence he may have manifested at his work.

(a) Throughout the course the classes, which are not to contain more than thirty or forty boys, are to be so graded that each will have its own maximum and minimum amount of matter to be seen, and the professor is strictly required to note the fact. Thus there is no cramming, no trespassing, no mincing, and hence no confusion. A chief function of the Head Master of the schools, whether high or low, is to see to the observance of this point. (b) The method of instruction is oral. There is an advantage in its being so, as it enables teachers the more readily to impress upon education those interesting features with which nothing but the living voice can invest it. Moreover, it brings them into nearer contact with their pupils, and helps to throw into bolder relief and with tangible results that paternal relationship which should exist between teacher and taught. As a feature of education, paternalism was always prized by the Jesuits, who looked upon it as necessary in practice if one is ever to acquire a knowledge of his pupils' character, which is, indeed, requisite for their proper moulding. It is a gratifying sign in the education of our day, that it is coming more into general favor, and the distance which has hitherto separated tutor from scholar is being gradually bridged over.[1]   (c) In the lower courses the

_____

(1) " Another reform introduced, but only begun to be carried out, is the establishment of a right relation between teacher and pupil.   They need to come

lessons are to be short, as every word, phrase and sentence is to be analyzed. Thoroughness is sought for above all else.[1] That the brighter or more diligent may not have idle time on their hands, a class of "Honors" is provided in each form in which special work is done, and which only those attend who surpass in the ordinary lessons. This device enables all to see as much matter as their talents warrant, without forcing the less gifted to undertake what is beyond their reach. (d) The various languages are to be studied in their

---

nearer to one another. Many of our primary schools are about models in this, but in higher forms a great gap between teacher and taught still yawns. They ought to approach each other closer in what I may call an ethical way, as well as in an intellectual way. We need, more than we have as yet done, to get upon a level of friendship with our pupils, not standing off from them, not looking down upon them. Present yourself to your pupils as their guide, friend, adviser, elder brother, one who, having the advantage of age and longer study, is able to assist them. The *in loco parentis* idea of the teacher's office is sometimes urged as an argument in favor of pedagogical sternness and severity. Not so. Parental authority itself is no longer exercised in the old way How many civilized fathers horsewhip their boys nowadays? In the lower grades, and, to an extent, in all, authority must exist, but it must be kept as much as possible in the background. Never coerce a pupil save as a last resort." *The next steps forward in Education,* by President Andrews. Brown University; in School and College. Vol. I. p. 5.

(1) "Stude potius," says Sacchini, "ut pauciora distincteque percipiant quam obscure atque confuse pluribus imbuantur." Or, as Macaulay puts it; "It will be found more nutritious to digest a page than to devour a volume." Essays. *Athenian Orators.*

respective classics rather than in grammars, rhetorics and mere compilations of literary odds and ends. Cicero is to be the Latin model all through the course, some of his easier treatises not being too difficult even for beginners when Masters do their duty by strict fidelity to the requirements of the daily *prælectio*. A very important ruling this, we think, and one too apt to be overlooked, particularly in the study of the vernacular. Yet, as a matter of indisputable fact, to illustrate from our own language, there is, as we know, infinitely more to be gleaned from a judicious reading of a single classic, be it a novel of Thackeray or Scott, or a poem of Tennyson, than can ever be hoped for from mere rule and rote begotten of dry, uninteresting abstractions. Nor do we say this in disparagement of precepts, but simply because we are persuaded that the major portion of a student's time should be devoted to authors as the chief means of improvement, and not to text-books, as is too frequently the case. (e) In the forms below *Rhetoric* there are to be four or five hours of class a-day. The order of exercises in the schoolroom is as follows: 1. *Recitation* of

the lessons given the previous day.
2. *Explanation* of the new lesson in *precepts*, of which the student must give a brief account to the teacher as soon as it is finished. This to rivet attention and secure results. 3. *Correction* of the exercises assigned the day before, and collected at the opening of class. 4. *Explanation* of the new lesson in the *Author* followed immediately by a repetition of the same, and preceded by a repetition of the *prælectio* of the day before. (f) Various means are resorted to in order to quicken the ambition or indolence of youth, as the case may be. Besides the public displays (*concertationes*) attended by only a limited number of classes, there are others at which the entire college, Faculty and pupils, is present; and others again, occurring several times a year, at which the parents of the students and the general public assist. The results of competitive exercises held in all the classes are proclaimed upon these occasions and premiums and other distinctions are bestowed upon the worthy. Again, semi-annual examinations are held in all the classes, and the results published and recorded. They determine

whether a student's present attainments justify his continuance in the class; whether, perhaps, it might not be better either to promote him in consideration of his rapid progress, or lower his grade, because of serious deficiency in the preceding term. Furthermore, Debating Societies and "Academies," as they are called, are organized under the supervision and immediate direction of some member of the Faculty. They serve as a vent for the growing information of the youthful mind consequent upon private reading and collateral study. As they enjoy a certain prestige, membership in them is reckoned an honor, and bestowed only upon the diligent and deserving. (g) Lastly, that the teachers themselves may always act in concert, monthly and daily conferences or meetings are provided for, in which a general interchange of view keeps every one posted on the drift of collegiate affairs. The *System* has other detailed features which would illustrate still further to what a minute extent the principles of organization have been carried out. Such as we have given, however, will suffice for present purposes. Speaking upon this subject, Ranke says: "They (the Jesuits) began by the closest observance of a carefully considered system, dividing the schools into classes, and pursuing in them a method strictly uniform, from the earliest principles of learning to the highest degree of science."[1] "No other school system," says Quick, "has been built up by the united efforts of so many astute intellects; no other system has met with so great success or attained such widespread influence."[2]

IV. Finally. Perhaps there was nothing more conducive to the popularity enjoyed by the Jesuits as educators than the prominence which they gave in their system to *moral training*.[3] Though we mention it

(1) Hist. of the Papacy. Vol. I. B. II. §. 7. He says again : "With them (the Jesuits) all was nicely calculated, every movement and action had its definite end and aim ; such combination of learning sufficing to its purpose with unswerving zeal, of studies and persuasion, of pomp and asceticism, of widely extended influence and unity in the governing principle and intention, has never been witnessed in the world before or since." Ibid. B. V. §. 3.

"The past as well as the present organization of the schools of the Jesuits," says Barnard, "the course of instruction, methods of teaching, and discipline, are worthy of profound study by teachers and educators who would profit by the experience of wise and learned men." *American Journal of Education.* Vol. V. p. 215. *Editorial Remark.*

(2) *Educational Reformers*, ut supra. pg. 20.

(3) "They (the Jesuits) paid great attention to the moral culture, and formed their pupils to good character and correct manners. * * * * From the

last, it was nevertheless considered by them the supreme element in education. The riotous, dissolute manner of life which disgraced the medieval universities was the bane of the day as everybody knows. So impressed was Ignatius by the dangers of the situation that he sought to provide a check and remedy by making the moral training of youth the essential object of his Institution. He did not fail to mark, nor his followers after him, the radical distinction between education and mere instruction. Education, as he understood it, meant the development of the whole man, and, therefore, aimed

Jesuits education received that tone of religion by which it has since been marked." Ranke. Hist. of the Papacy. Vol. I. B. V. 2. 3.

In remarkable contrast with this statement of a non-Catholic, but recognized authority, is the declaration of Samuel Williams, Ph. D., who has lately written what may be justly styled one of the most ludicrous parodies upon the "History of Modern Education" that has been floated upon the market for years. Speaking of the educational work of the Jesuits and without, of course, adducing any proof of his assertions and insinuations, he says: "Originality or independence of thought was no part of their object, nor was it encouraged. From the narrowness of aim and from the alleged lack of deep morality based on principle which their system inculcated, sprang the faults with which the education they give is charged." The entire work teems with similar shallow absurdities, so bald and unsubstantiated that they can serve no other purpose than to emphasize the utter incompetency or blind fanaticism of the author.

History of Modern Education, by Samuel Williams, Ph. D.; C. W. Bardeen, Syracuse, N. Y.

primarily at the formation of character as being the most essential part of that development. Such a formation mere intellectual cultivation could never bring about, for the obvious reason that it never touches the domain of morals except speculatively, and exercises no determining influence upon the practice and purposes of life. And character, he was convinced, without a moral substructure, were as inconceivable as daylight with the sun blotted from the heavens. Accordingly, great as might be their zeal for mental improvement, his followers were to be infinitely more concerned about the formation of the hearts of their pupils Development of character along the lines of a sturdy moral growth was to take precedence of everything else.[1] And in this wise

---

(1) "Speaking succinctly," says President Andrews, "the constituents of a sound education are first, character; second, culture; third, critical power, including accuracy and also sympathy with all the various ages, nationalities and moods of men; and fourth, power to work hard under rule and pressure. We see that here mere knowledge is left out of the account. It 's quite incidental and relatively insig nificant. Yet this is what most people have been wont to regard as the sum and substance of education. * * * * The definition makes character part of education and even gives it the first place. All reflecting persons are coming t﹖ feel that unless schooling makes pupils morally better, purer within and sweeter, kinder, stronger in outward conduct, it is unworthy the name." *Ut supra.* How refreshing

provision we see the real germ-motive of all their energy—the mainspring of an activity so restless that to some minds, unable to comprehend it, it savored of genuine fanaticism. They scouted danger and underwent every hardship for the privilege of being allowed to mould the undeveloped mind and heart. The work might be difficult; the results in many cases scant. The very ones in whose interest their zeal was being exercised might prove callous to the efforts being made in their behalf. Yet they were never to falter. Neither were they to look upon those efforts as wholly profitless, so long as they succeeded in making their pupils better citizens and Christians by rooting them still more firmly in the love and service of God. With this end in view, religion was ever kept in the foreground. Its vital importance as a factor in education was insisted upon whenever opportunity offered. Practical instructions covering the dogmas of revelation were given at stated intervals, thus supplying the young mind with the logical groundwork of the faith to

in an age that has gone mad on book learning to hear one of our leading educators sounding a note so deep and full and true.

which it clung, as well as the arms with which to meet in successful conflict the attacks that would inevitably·be made upon it later. That practice might tally with theory, and the soul be put in closer touch with its Maker than by mere abstract speculations, numerous pious exercises were prescribed which served as timely reminders to the students of the higher and more arduous work which they had in hand, the assimilation, namely, into the practice of daily individual life of the evangelical precepts and of the virtues of Him of whose character those precepts are the living and glorious embodiment.[1] Daily Mass, prayers at the opening and closing of schools, the frequentation of the Sacraments, and the institution of religious confraternities to which only students who excelled in deportment were eligible, all pointed in this direction —conspiring to a common result. Moreover, the reading of the students was carefully supervised, and

---

(1) Nor is the zeal displayed in this matter a thing of the past. " In scholis etiam nostris," says the late General, Very Rev. A. M. Anderledy, in a recent encyclical letter to the members of his Order, "coelesti huic doctrinae primas dari necesse est, atque ita dari, ut persuasum sit omnibus, vitam ad Christi Domini norman exigendam in summa apud nos laude poni atque honore."

nothing that could dim the lustre of youthful innocence was ever allowed to reach them. Pagan authors, though read in class, were diligently expurgated, while much of the current folly masquerading under the name of "literature of the day," was kept at a safe and remote distance. Add to all which constant and intimate intercourse, upon the play ground as well as in the class-room, with men wholly given over to the service of God, and we readily perceive how salutary, how elevating must have been the atmosphere in which their young lives were to grow and prosper. So important a part, in fact, was religious training to play that the *Ratio* gives very minute instructions to Masters on the care they are to take of their pupils, of the flawless example they are to set them, and of the unalterable patience and weariless solicitude they are to exercise in dealing with them, ever mindful of the sentiment of the poet:

"Nemo adeo ferus est, ut non mitescere
    possit,
  Si modo culturae patientem commodet
    aurem."[1]

---

(1) Horace. Epist. i. V. 39.

A religious training characterized by so much assiduity and system and continued throughout the formative period of life must have had, in the very nature of things, a telling influence, and that influence beneficial upon the moral make-up of the students. This is not the place nor do we consider it worth the while to examine the charge, now quite threadbare, that Jesuit influence was morally deleterious. It needs no refutation. It was one of the numerous slanders perpetrated at the expense of the Order by its adversaries in former days. The vindictive raciness of Pascal, Arnaud and others was enlisted to invest it with the charm of rare wit and genius. Trumped up by vilifiers, like every calumny it lived its little day until other and better tactics supplanted it in the field of upright polemics. A wiser than Solomon has said, ''by their fruits you shall know them,'' and a system which could give birth to men of the princely mould of Francis De Sales, Alphonsus Liguori, Tasso, Benedict XIV, Bossuet, Leo XIII, and a whole army of others has no apology to offer for its moral character.[1] If

(1) Histoire de la Compagnie de Jésus, par Crétineau-Joly, Vol. 4, p. 207.

in their youth the lives of such men
had been polluted they could never
have bequeathed to posterity so many
memorials of character framed upon
principles as broad as they are sound.
X Not every Jesuit pupil, it must be
confessed, in the three hundred years
of their history has been a credit to
his tutors.    Neither was it to have
been expected.    But the fault was
not the Society's.    Even the most
celebrated of those who played it
false and perhaps the most pro-
nounced in his antagonism, the
famous Voltaire, admits as much,
and describes in no doubtful terms
his own estimate of the lives of men
whose morality and God-fearing
spirit he could praise while not car-
ing to imitate them.    ''During the
seven years,'' he writes, ''that I
lived in the house of the Jesuits,
what did I see amongst them?    The
most laborious, frugal and regular
life ; all their hours divided between
the care they spent on us and the
exercises of their austere profession.
I attest the same as thousands of
others brought up by them, like my-
self ; not one will be found to con-
tradict me. - Hence I can never cease
wondering how any one can accuse

them of teaching corrupt morality.ᛉ
*  *  *  *  Let any one place
side by side the *Provincial Letters* and
the sermons of Father Bourdaloue: he
will learn in the former the art of
raillery, the art of presenting things,
indifferent in themselves, under as-
pects which make them appear crim-
inal, the art of insulting with elo-
quence ; he will learn from Father
Bourdaloue that of being severe to
oneself and indulgent to others."[1]
So spoke Voltaire, and it is only to
be regretted that a seed so precious
should have fallen upon a heart so
irresponsive.

✝ These we think, not to mention
others of less importance, were the
principal reasons for the popularity
and consequent influence enjoyed by
the Society of Jesus as an educational
body.  They filled a need of the
times and it was quite to be expected
that the Institute of Ignatius should
have been welcomed as a step in advance of the old order of things, and
as more in harmony with the spirit
of an age that was gradually break-
ing with the traditional and narrow
conservatism of the past.  In the

---

(1) Lettre 7 février 1746.   Tom. VIII. p. 1128.
Edit. 1817.

sunshine of the favor thus vouchsafed it, the Order grew rapidly as history universally attests; and that its course in future, under similar circumstances, would have been equally prosperous and speedy there was every reason to believe. But all this time its enemies had not been idle. They had multiplied and compassed it round about. They were instant in their demands for its suppression, and their clamors eventually prevailed. One word from the Vicar of Christ was all that was needed, and, as we know, it was spoken; and upon its single utterance the Society of Jesus and its world-wide educational influence passed away. But in the rulings of a higher destiny the fatality was to be of short duration. Yet awhile it would reappear clothed with its ancient life and vigor and prepared once more to resume its former work in the field of pedagogics—when the power that smote it unto death would bid it wake again.

www.ingramcontent.com/pod-product-compliance
Lightning Source LLC
Chambersburg PA
CBHW021520090426
42739CB00007B/694